Pebble® Plus

Patterns in Nature

Hibernation

by Margaret Hall

Consulting Editor: Gail Saunders-Smith, PhD

Content Consultant: Dr. Ronald Browne, Associate Professor of Elementary Education
Minnesota State University, Mankato, Minnesota

Capstone press®

Mankato, Minnesota

Pebble Plus is published by Capstone Press,
151 Good Counsel Drive, P.O. Box 669, Mankato, Minnesota 56002.
www.capstonepress.com

1 2 3 4 5 6 11 10 09 08 07 06

Library of Congress Cataloging-in-Publication Data
Hall, Margaret, 1947–
    Hibernation / by Margaret Hall.
        p. cm.— (Pebble plus. Patterns in nature)
    Includes bibliographical references (p. 23) and index.
    ISBN-13: 978-0-7368-6339-1 (hardcover)   978-0-7368-7540-0 (softcover)
    ISBN-10: 0-7368-6339-7 (hardcover)   0-7368-7540-9 (softcover)
    1. Hibernation—Juvenile literature. I. Title. II. Series.
QL755.H35 2007
591.56'5—dc22   2006001453

Summary: Simple text and photographs introduce hibernation and how some animals prepare for and
    experience hibernation each year.

Editorial Credits
Heather Adamson, editor; Kia Adams, designer; Jo Miller, photo researcher/photo editor

Photo Credits
Corbis/George McCarthy, 7, 21 (dormouse peering from hole and dormouse hibernating in nest); Hans Dieter
    Brandi/Frank Lane Picture Agency, 21 (dormouse eating berry); Hal Beral, cover (bear catching fish);
    Kennan Ward, 1, 11; Arthur Morris, cover (bear eating); zefa/E. & P. Bauer, cover (bear sleeping)
Dwight R. Kuhn, 13
Nature Picture Library/Colin Preston, 21 (dormouse on bramble)
NHPA/Anthony Bannister, 17
Peter Arnold/Deborah Allen, 19; S. J. Krasemann, 9
Photo Researchers Inc./Anne Fournier, 15
Shutterstock/Juerg Schreiter, backcover
SuperStock, 5

Note to Parents and Teachers

The Patterns in Nature set supports national science standards related to earth
and life science. This book describes and illustrates hibernation. The images support
early readers in understanding the text. The repetition of words and phrases helps early
readers learn new words. This book also introduces early readers to subject-specific
vocabulary words, which are defined in the Glossary section. Early readers may need
assistance to read some words and to use the Table of Contents, Glossary, Read More,
Internet Sites, and Index sections of the book.

Table of Contents

Why Hibernate?

Winter weather can be
cold, cold, cold.
Food is hard to find.
Every winter, some animals
stay alive by hibernating.

Hibernating animals take
a long, sleepy rest.
They breathe slowly.
Their hearts beat slowly too.
They need less food for
energy and heat.

True hibernators, like bats,
sleep snuggled in for weeks
without waking.
They don't eat. They don't
even go to the bathroom.

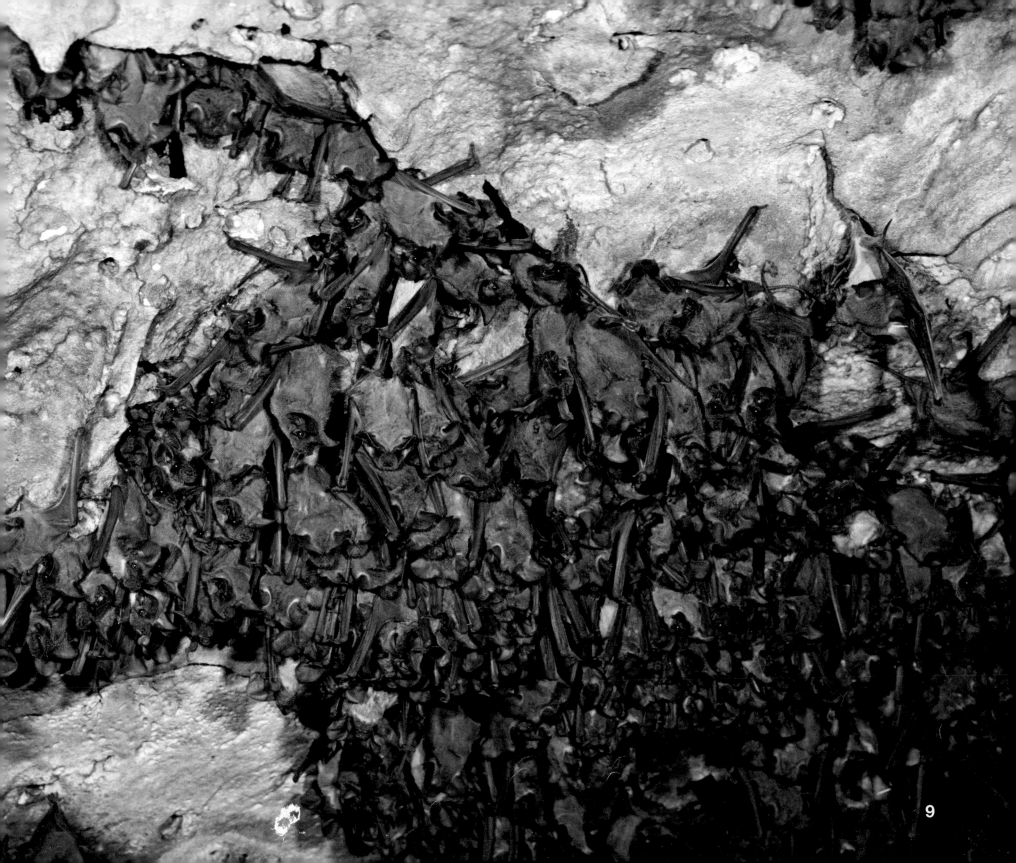

9

Getting Ready

Animals eat extra food before
they hibernate.
Bears get very fat in fall.
They won't eat much
during winter.

Some animals store up food
near their beds.
Chipmunks wake up
and search for a snack of
hidden nuts. Then they go
back to sleep.

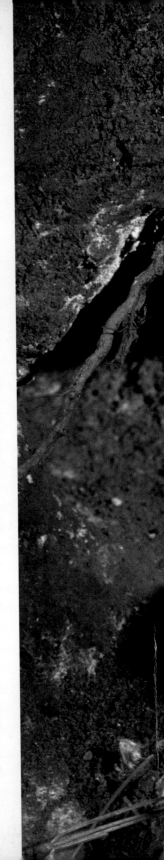

A Place to Rest

Groundhogs hibernate
underground in burrows.
Squirrels rest in nests
made of leaves.

Frogs dig down deep and
sleep tucked in the mud.
Snakes curl up together
in caves.

Finally, the cold winter
months end and spring comes
again. Hungry animals leave
their winter beds
to look for food.

It's a Pattern

Hibernating is one

of nature's patterns.

When winter returns, animals

will hibernate once again.

Getting Ready

Finding a Den

**Leaving
the Den**

Hibernating

21

Glossary

burrow—a tunnel or hole in the ground made or used by an animal

energy—the strength to do active things; food is needed to make energy in living creatures.

hibernate—to spend winter in a sleepy resting state without much activity

pattern—something that happens again and again in the same order

true hibernator—a hibernating animal that spends much of the winter in a sleeplike state and does not wake for weeks at a time; true hibernators have low body temperatures and heart rates; small mammals such as dormice and bats are true hibernators.

Read More

Ganeri, Anita. *Hibernation*. Nature's Patterns. Chicago: Heinemann, 2005.

Murphy, Patricia J. *Why Do Some Animals Hibernate?* The Library of Why Series. New York: PowerKids Press, 2004.

Scrace, Carolyn. *Hibernation*. Cycles of Life. New York: Franklin Watts, 2002.

Internet Sites

FactHound offers a safe, fun way to find Internet sites related to this book. All of the sites on FactHound have been researched by our staff.

Here's how:

1. Visit *www.facthound.com*

2. Choose your grade level.

3. Type in this book ID **0736863397** for age-appropriate sites. You may also browse subjects by clicking on letters, or by clicking on pictures and words.

4. Click on the **Fetch It** button.

FactHound will fetch the best sites for you!

Index

Word Count: 170
Grade: 1
Early-Intervention Level: 16